MW01356972

discovermore

Life in a Community

Community Resources

Dwayne Hicks

IN ASSOCIATION WITH

Published in 2024 by Britannica Educational Publishing (a trademark of Encyclopædia Britannica, Inc.) in association with
The Rosen Publishing Group, Inc.
2544 Clinton Street, Buffalo, NY 14224

Distributed exclusively by Rosen Publishing.
To see additional Britannica Educational Publishing titles, go to rosenpublishing.com.

Editor: Kathleen Klatte
Book Design: Leslie Taylor

Photo Credits: Cover Bobex-73/Shutterstock.com; (series background) Dai Yim/Shutterstock.com; p. 4 Goinyk Production/Shutterstock.com; p. 5 Sean Locke Photography/Shutterstock.com; p. 7 (top) Tap10/Shutterstock.com, (bottom) Oleggg/Shutterstock.com; p. 8 Dalibor Sevaljevic/Shutterstock.com; p. 9 junpiiiiiiiiiii/Shutterstock.com; p. 10 agrofruti/Shutterstock.com; p. 11 Boyd Hendrikse/Shutterstock.com; p. 12 Rich Carey/Shutterstock.com; p. 13 fokke baarssen/Shutterstock.com; p. 14 Bjoern Wylezich/Shutterstock.com; p. 15 Vyacheslav Svetlichnyy/Shutterstock.com; p. 17 (top) Mikadun/Shutterstock.com, (bottom) Videohotdogs/Shutterstock.com; p. 18 Bruceton/Shutterstock.com; p. 19 Mike Shooter/Shutterstock.com; p. 20 Avim Wu/Shutterstock.com; p. 21 sirtravelalot/Shutterstock.com; p. 22 pikselstock/Shutterstock.com; p. 23 Andrew F. Kazmierski/Shutterstock.com; p. 24 MindStorm/Shutterstock.com; p. 25 RozenskiP/Shutterstock.com; p. 26 wavebreakmedia/Shutterstock.com; p. 27 Prostock-studio/Shutterstock.com; p. 29 (top) Krunja/Shutterstock.com, p. 29 (bottom) Rawpixel.com/Shutterstock.com.

Cataloging-in-Publication Data

Names: Hicks, Dwayne.
Title: Community resources / Dwayne Hicks.
Description: New York : Britannica Educational Publishing, in Association with Rosen Educational Services. 2024. | Series: Discover more: life in a community | Includes glossary and index.
Identifiers: ISBN 9781642828757 (library bound) | ISBN 9781642828740 (pbk) | ISBN 9781642828764 (ebook)
Subjects: LCSH: Communities--Environmental aspects--Juvenile literature. | Community development--Environmental aspects--Juvenile literature. | Natural resources--Juvenile literature.
Classification: LCC HM756.H53 2024 | DDC 307–dc23

Manufactured in the United States of America

Some of the images in this book illustrate individuals who are models. The depictions do not imply actual situations or events.

CPSIA Compliance Information: Batch #CSBRIT24. For further information contact Rosen Publishing at 1-800-237-9932.

Contents

Components of a Community

Community resources are all the things available for members of a community to use. They can include the people of the community, goods and services, and natural resources.

The most important part of a community is the people who are in it. Community members might live near each other, be close in age, or speak the same language. Being part of a community means that individuals are surrounded by those who care for them.

A tree can be used for lumber or firewood. It can also be used to manufacture paper.

Police officers provide a community service. They are trained to keep their communities safe.

Goods are items you can touch, like food, clothing, and furniture. They are either grown or made from raw materials. Services are actions that people do for someone else. Services include delivering mail, repairing cars, and teaching classes.

Natural resources are things found in nature that people can use. Some natural resources are used by themselves. Others are combined to manufacture new resources.

WORD WISE

A community is a group of people who live in the same area and rely on the same resources.

Creating Wealth

Some communities are able to provide all the goods and services their residents need. Others might need to sell or exchange with people in different communities. Either way, wealth is created. Wealth is all things that have value when they are exchanged. The greater a community's wealth, the more it can offer its members.

The people in a community are also a kind of resource. A community might not have its own police or fire department, hospital, or airport. But it could still have caring people who help each other. For example, neighborhood communities will always be important for people like single parents and older adults. Older people often rely on others in the community to bring them meals or check that they're OK during severe weather.

A farmer is selling a cow. He'll use the money from that sale to buy new equipment for his farm.

compare and contrast

During the COVID-19 pandemic, many people relied on the services of delivery people to obtain goods for their homes. Now they can go out to local shops again. Which do you think is better? Why?

Now the farmer can buy a new tractor. The tractor salesman will have money to buy more stock for his store.

Where Does It All Come From?

Production is the process of combining raw materials to make new things. There are three major factors in production. The first is land. Land can mean the ground where a business is located. A business can be a large farm or a tiny workshop. Land also includes natural resources. Natural resources are all the things that nature gives us. All goods come from the land in one way or another.

Skilled sheep shearers use simple tools to obtain wool.

Other trained workers will use more complicated tools to spin, dye, and weave the wool into cloth.

The workers are the second factor of production. This includes their skills and knowledge about their jobs. Nothing can be created, sold, or used without people to make it happen.

The third part of production is capital. Capital includes all the human-made resources used to make and provide the goods and services. Capital can be as simple as a hammer and nails, or as complex as a factory run by computers.

Consider This

You probably have a warm wool hat for winter. What natural resources do you think went into making that hat? What kind of tools were used? What skills and knowledge were needed?

Natural Resources

Planet Earth is an amazing place. It provides everything humans need to live. Examples are soil, light, water, plants, animals, minerals, and air. These natural resources can be used as food, fuel, or clothing. Some are used as raw materials to make other things.

Apples are a natural resource. They can be enjoyed raw, cooked, or as juice.

Consider This

Suppose you were going to live on a space station. How would you make up for the lack of natural resources?

Beautiful rock formations are also natural resources. People like to visit them. This can provide income for a community.

Some communities have many natural resources. They may have good land and plenty of water for farming. Other communities may have minerals that can be made into products. The products can be sold to bring in money for the community. Some places have areas of natural beauty where people in the community enjoy spending time. Other places do not have many natural resources. People who live there may need to trade with other communities for food or materials to make things.

Renewable Resources

Apple trees produce a new crop of fruit every year. Sheep grow more wool and have more lambs. This type of natural resource is called renewable. They can be replaced or used again.

Plants and animals are renewable natural resources because they reproduce, or make more of their own kind. After crops like wheat and corn are grown and collected, more wheat and corn can be planted. The same is true for trees. They can be cut down and used to make furniture or houses. More trees can be planted to replace the ones that were cut down.

Trees are a renewable resource, but they can take a long time to grow back. When too many are cut down too quickly, the soil can be damaged.

Wind can be used to move wind turbines, or windmills, which then creates electricity.

Sunlight, wind, **geotherma**l (heat) energy, and biofuels are renewable, too. We can use them without worrying that they will run out. We still have to take good care of renewable resources.

WORD WISE

Geothermal energy comes from the heat of Earth's interior.

Running On Empty

Some natural resources took millions of years to form. There are only certain amounts of them in the earth. They are nonrenewable because they cannot be replaced once they are used. Rock, minerals, metals, and fossil fuels are all nonrenewable. Fossil fuels are natural substances made from the remains of plants and animals that lived millions of years ago. Natural gas, petroleum (oil), and coal are fossil fuels.

Diamonds are valuable because they're rare. It can take one billion years for a diamond to form!

Digging for coal is hard work. Miners can get sick from breathing coal dust.

People use fossil fuels every day. They use them to heat buildings, make electricity, cook, and run machines. They use gasoline and plastic made from petroleum. Many things made from petroleum don't decompose or break down after they're used. They create pollution that damages Earth.

Consider This

Open your refrigerator and look inside. How many things are sold in plastic containers? What happens to those containers once they're empty?

Water, Water Everywhere!

Water covers most of the Earth's surface. It renews itself through the water cycle. When liquid water in oceans, rivers, and lakes warms up, it turns into water vapor. Water vapor is an invisible gas that floats into the air. As it rises, it cools and becomes tiny droplets. These droplets form clouds. Later, they fall back to the ground as rain or snow. This cycle means water can be used over and over.

But not every community has access to good water. Many people have to dig wells to get water from deep underground. It takes a long time to replace that water through the water cycle. Some scientists say groundwater is not as renewable as we once thought. We have to be careful to keep our precious water supply clean and safe for drinking.

The ocean and falling rain are liquid water. The clouds are made of gaseous water.

compareandcontrast

If you live in a city or large town, your water flows through pipes from a water treatment plant. But what if you lived far away from the nearest town? Where do you think your water would come from?

This water is full of garbage. Does it look safe to drink? Do you think anything can live in it?

Protecting Our Future

Communities need access to natural resources to thrive. Sometimes, however, getting at those resources can cause problems. The process can harm the environment. Also, if nonrenewable resources are used up, they will be gone forever.

These deer are eating someone's garden because human activity destroyed their habitat. Now they're considered a nuisance.

Oil damages the feathers of aquatic birds. It also kills many of the things they eat.

To access natural resources, such as fossil fuels, people often dig or drill into the ground. The mines or wells they make can cause land to erode, or wear away. They often leave behind piles of waste. Sometimes, oil is spilled that destroys wildlife. When fossil fuels like coal and petroleum are burned, they release chemicals. This harms the air, water, and soil.

Clearing land for buildings or farms can wipe out forests. Animals then are forced to move from their homes. Sometimes whole species of animals become extinct due to human activity.

Consider This

An oil spill affects the community on many levels. Polluted water isn't safe to swim in or pretty to look at, so tourist money is lost. Fish and other animals that people like to eat are killed, affecting the food industry. What other impacts can you think of?

Cleaning Up After Ourselves

When people around the world realized how badly we were using up our natural resources, they started thinking of ways to save them. This is known as conservation.

Every year, the U.S. state of Virginia hosts "Clean the Bay Day." Thousands of people participate in the event and clean trash from Chesapeake Bay and its shores.

Some artists specialize in making sculptures from recycled plastic.

Used glass containers can be recycled into new glass.

In the province of Buriram, Thailand, the sarus crane (a kind of bird) had died out because rice farmers there used pesticides and noisy tractors. Sarus cranes are an **endangered species**. Scientists brought some of the cranes from another country and released them in Buriram. The farmers helped the birds survive by parking their noisy tractors and switching to organic farming. Organic farming is a method of farming that does not use chemicals.

People throughout the world participate in recycling programs. People set aside glass, plastic, and paper. These items are taken to a recycling center to be processed into new ones.

WORD WISE

An endangered species is a kind of animal or plant that's become very rare and might die out completely.

Moving From Place to Place

All communities need to be able to move goods and people from place to place. Most communities build transportation systems to help their members get around. Transportation is all the ways people move themselves and goods from one place to another.

In some communities, people use bikes more often than cars. This means less gas is used and less pollution is produced.

Railway stations are important to a community. People can move from place to place or even eat or shop.

Communities usually provide sidewalks and roads. They build bridges and tunnels to make transportation easier. They have railroads for trains and docks for ships. Sometimes, they build airports, highways, and public systems like subways and bus systems.

A community's economy depends on transportation. Raw materials must be moved from where they are found to factories. Then, products must travel from factories to stores. Food, minerals, wood, and other natural resources often travel by truck, railroad, or ship. People use transportation within their own community and between other communities.

Consider This

Think about all the different ways you move around your community. How do you get to school? To the store? To the movies?

What Else Do Communities Need?

Most communities offer services and facilities to keep things safe and comfortable for the people who live there. Together, these are called the infrastructure. The infrastructure includes all the community's public buildings and roads. Public utilities are also part of the infrastructure.

In many communities, you will find schools, libraries, museums, banks, hospitals, and government buildings.

The Bronx Zoo in New York occupies half of a city park.

Communities employ people to keep the roads safe.

Police and fire departments protect people and property. Dams and levees control water and flooding. Other human-made resources can include everything from loading docks and storage tanks to recycling centers and homeless shelters.

Some communities have park systems and recreation centers where people go to exercise, play sports, and have fun. Communities may provide walking and bike trails, soccer fields, and baseball diamonds. Large communities might have skating rinks, swimming pools, or even zoos.

Consider This

In most communities, the Department of Public Works (DPW) is part of the local government. They're responsible for things like cleaning streets and collecting trash and recycling. What would happen in your community if the DPW didn't do its job on a daily basis?

Human Resources

The people who work in a community are one of its most important resources. People are paid for their work, then they spend money in the community for goods and services they need or want. Each year in September, the United States honors workers with a holiday. Labor Day reminds us that the labor force helps improve lives in the community.

There are many kinds of jobs. For example, when you think about a factory, you might think first of workers who make the factory products.

Everyone's job is important. If there were no goods on the shelves, or the store was dirty, would you want to shop there?

These people are volunteering their time to pick up litter. This helps make the community a nicer place for everyone who lives there.

But there are also supervisors in charge of the work. Some workers repair the machines and check on safety, while others deliver the products once they are made. All the workers have special skills.

Men and women who do not have jobs that pay wages are an asset to the community as well. They care for their homes and families. **Volunteers** are an important part of a community. They might do things like bring meals to elderly people or read to kids at the library.

WORD WISE

A volunteer is a person who does work without being paid for it.

With a Little Help From Our Friends

Sometimes a community isn't able to provide everything its members need. It might not have the right resources or enough people to do the work. Besides the things they need, there might be goods or services that people would enjoy. To solve this problem, communities trade with each other.

Trade is the business of buying and selling items. Resources of all types can be traded. Those resources then can be used to make products that can be sold in other places. Improved transportation and advancements in computer science have made trade between communities easier than ever.

Trade creates jobs. Jobs provide paychecks to the workers and their families. They then use their money to buy more goods and services. Trade within a community and between communities helps build a strong economy.

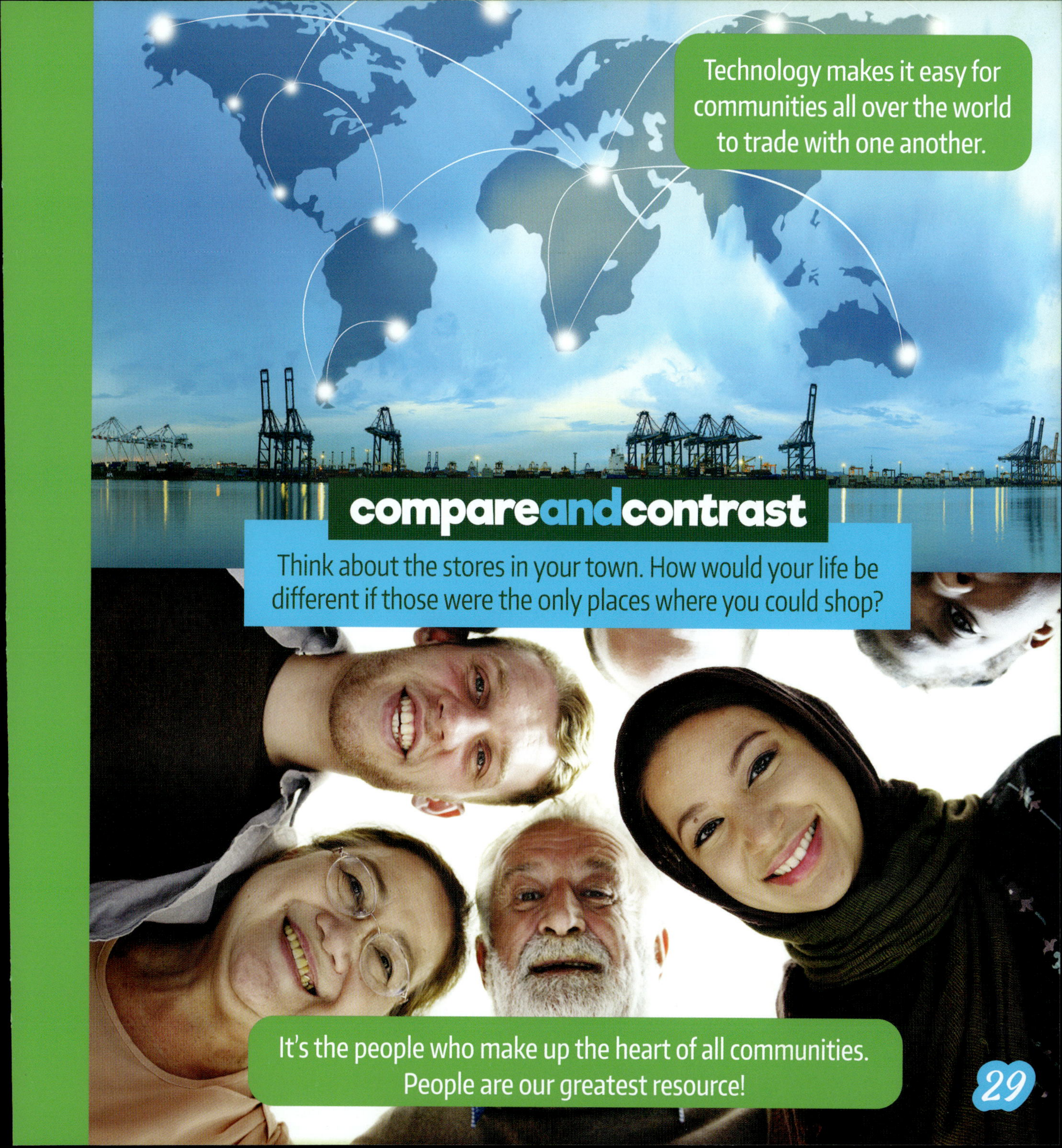
Technology makes it easy for communities all over the world to trade with one another.
compareandcontrast
Think about the stores in your town. How would your life be different if those were the only places where you could shop?
It's the people who make up the heart of all communities. People are our greatest resource!

Glossary

biofuels: A fuel (such as wood or ethanol) composed of or produced from biological raw materials.

economy: The process or system by which goods and services are produced, sold, and bought in a country or region.

environment: All of the physical surroundings on Earth, including the air, water, soil, plants, and animals.

fossil fuels: Natural substances made from the remains of plants and animals that lived millions of years ago.

groundwater: Water found underground within cracks and spaces in soil, sand, and rock and that supplies wells and springs.

impact: To have a strong and often bad effect on (something or someone).

invisible: Impossible to see; not visible.

levee: A bank built along a river to prevent flooding.

manufacture: To make (something) usually in large amounts by using machines.

mineral: A substance that occurs naturally and is usually obtained from the ground.

nonrenewable resource: Something valuable found in nature that cannot be replaced once it is used up.

pesticide: A chemical that is used to kill animals or insects that damage plants or crops.

petroleum: An oily flammable liquid obtained from wells drilled in the ground; the source of gasoline, kerosene, and fuel oil.

raw materials: The basic material that can be used to make or create something.

renewable resource: Something valuable found in nature that can be replaced or grown back and used again.

For More Information

Books

123 Andrés. *Mi comunidad! My Community! (Spanish and English Edition)*. New York, NY: Scholastic Teaching Resources, 2021.

Brisson, Pat. *They're Heroes Too: A Celebration of Community.* Thomaston, ME: Tilbury House Publishers, 2022.

Websites

At-home Volunteer Activities for Kids
www.habitat.org/stories/home-volunteering-activities-kids
Habitat for Humanity has exercises kids can do at home to learn about housing, a critical community resource.

Community
www.timeforkids.com/k1/sections/community
Time for Kids has fun sections about the people, places, and things in a community.

Index